THIS BOOK BELONGS TO

_____

WELCOME TO OUR HOME!

Inspired by our brick-building-loving children, we have put together a series of activity books that families and friends would enjoy playing and learning together. Our two families have a total of five kids, aged three to nine years old. We have made it our mission to encourage our children to PLAY – LEARN – GROW!

Our fourth book - PETS - drew inspiration from our kids' love for all sorts of animals that they want to keep in the house! Our kids helped to pick their imaginary pets, named each animal and tested the brick builds; it is very important that our designs are kids-approved!

We have organized this book to be a tool for children aged four and up to learn key cognitive concepts, while the building processes encourage problem-solving skills. Check out pages 4 and 5 to find out more on how to use this book. Each entertaining new project gives children a sense of accomplishment — and offers them a new friend to play with.

Most of the bricks used in this book are from the Classic Lego boxes. Special pieces may be ordered easily online; here are three of our favorite sites:

Pick A Brick | LEGO Shop (https://shop.lego.com/pab)

Bricklink (https://www.bricklink.com/)

ToyPro (https://www.toypro.com/)

As your children learn while having fun, they will also be having a blast with their new pet pals. Let your children's imaginations run wild - change brick colors, add accessories, etc - encourage your children to think outside the box to make something truly spectacular!

From the parents of Caleb, Sofia, Joy, Natalie & Abby,

- Paul, Elaine, Ronald & Ann

Copyright © 2018 by Sofie & Nate Inc.
First published & printed in USA.
ISBN-13: 978-1983409479
ISBN-10: 1983409472
Designer: Paul Bacio
Co-Designer & Cover Illustrator: Sofia Chen
Layout & Page Design: Dan Pitts
Editorial Reviewer: Elaine Bacio
Project Editor: Ann Kositchotitana

TABLE OF CONTENTS

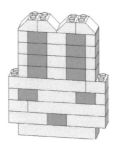

BUILDING BY PICTURES

This brick-building activity book shows you how to build 10 animals. Each activity shows all the bricks that you will need to build your animal. We show the build process in a step-by-step graphic guide and provide Red Arrow indicators that tell you where to put the bricks. This is an activity that you can do with family and friends. Have fun building your animal!
Woof-woof! Meow-meow! Squeak-squeak!

READY... GET SET... PLAY!

LEVEL INDICATOR

Three levels - EASY, MEDIUM, and ADVANCED - are presented. EASY is for children who are new to brick building. MEDIUM provides more challenging fun with more brick colors integration. ADVANCED involves more complex detailed brick building.

LEARNING CONCEPTS

Each activity has 3 to 4 specific concepts that are provided for parents/caretakers to integrate into their play with the child. Creative play helps with cognitive development. So play, learn, and grow!

THE FINISHED PRODUCT

The picture shows what the completely built animal looks like. You can also get creative and change colors of the bricks...and totally give your animal a unique look! Have fun!

BRICKS - PARTS LIST

All the bricks - colors, shapes, sizes, and quantities - needed to build the animals are listed here for easy reference. Sort the bricks so it will be easier to build later on.

CREATIVE PLAY

The concept of this book is simple. Using the directions provided, parents and caretakers can help their children build different animals out of bricks. These imaginative projects will help your entire family bond as your child has fun and absorbs a number of important developmental concepts. Incorporate learning into playtime as shown in this book—with fantastic results!

These activities will teach your children about the following:
* Recognizing and naming colors
* Familiarity with shapes such as square, rectangle, slopes, and so forth
* Counting objects and counting from 1 to 11
* Recognizing written numerals from 1 to 11
* Simple positioning concepts, such as top, bottom, over, under, beside, and so forth
* Simple directions in sequence (top-to-bottom, left-to-right)
* Sorting and grouping common objects by colors, shapes, and sizes

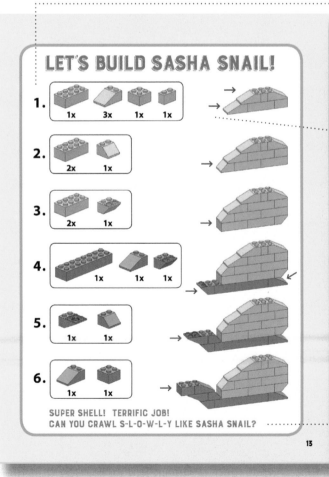

STEP-BY-STEP

Each step is detailed with the specific bricks that are needed for that step: colors, shapes, sizes, and quantities. This way, it is easier for the child to follow, be prepared, and not get frustrated.

RED ARROWS

The red arrows serve as visual direction cues to guide the child where to place the bricks.

ENCOURAGING WORDS

Words are powerful. Parents and caretakers can make this creative play activity more meaningful with encouraing words that cheer the child on in his/her building endeavor. A child may get stuck with certain steps; when this happens, you can encourage them to try different ways to solve the problem. Be sure to praise the child's effort at the end when he/she completes the animal!

HARRIET HAMSTER

Level: EASY

LEARNING CONCEPTS

1. Sort building bricks by color

2. Count the number of bricks in each color group

3. Understand the concepts of "Big" and "Small"

READY... GET SET... SORT!

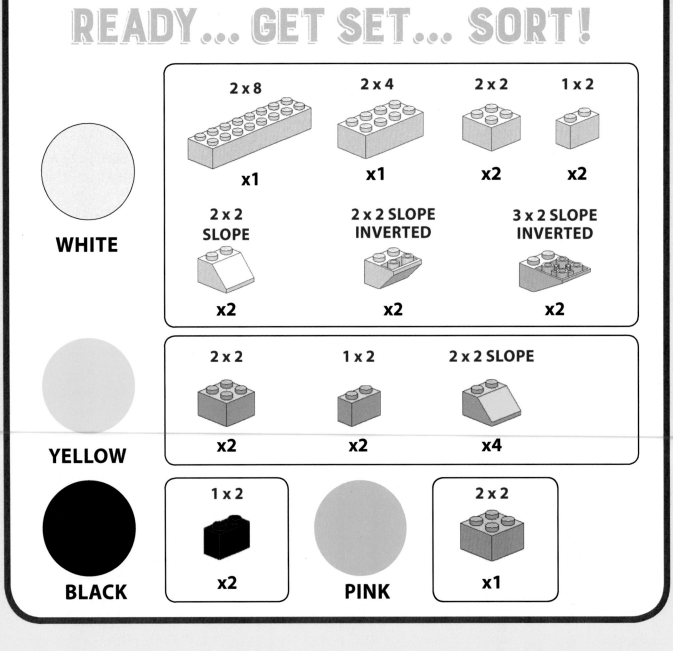

WHITE

2 x 8	2 x 4	2 x 2	1 x 2
x1	x1	x2	x2

2 x 2 SLOPE	2 x 2 SLOPE INVERTED	3 x 2 SLOPE INVERTED
x2	x2	x2

YELLOW

2 x 2	1 x 2	2 x 2 SLOPE
x2	x2	x4

BLACK

1 x 2
x2

PINK

2 x 2
x1

LET'S BUILD HARRIET HAMSTER!

1. 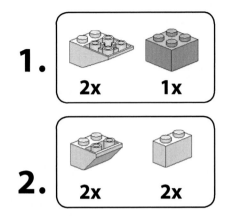 2x 1x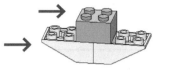

2. 2x 2x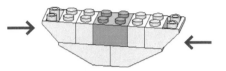

3. 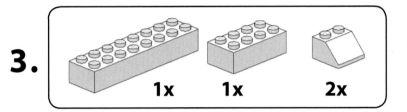 1x 1x 2x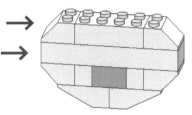

4. 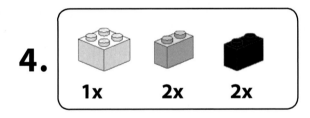 1x 2x 2x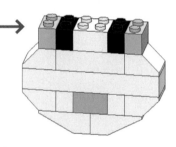

5. 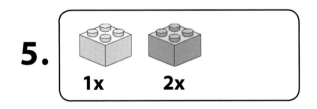 1x 2x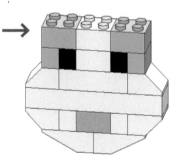

6. 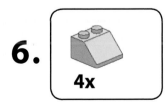 4x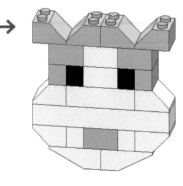

SUPER STAR! HARRIET HAMSTER LIKES
TO RUN. WHAT DO YOU LIKE TO DO?

BELINDA BUNNY

Level: EASY

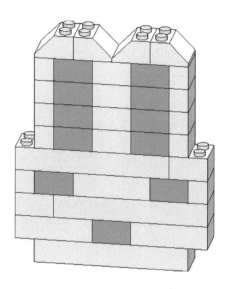

LEARNING CONCEPTS

1. Sort building bricks by color

2. Compare building bricks using the words "Longer" and "Shorter"

3. Follow directions using the words "Top," "Bottom," and "Next to"

READY... GET SET... SORT!

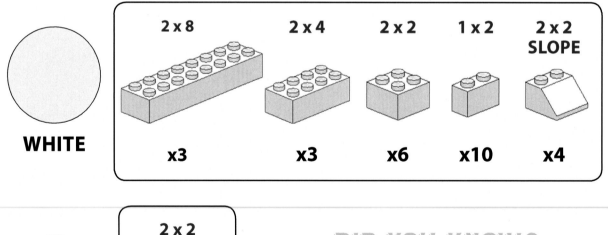

	2 x 8	2 x 4	2 x 2	1 x 2	2 x 2 SLOPE
WHITE	x3	x3	x6	x10	x4

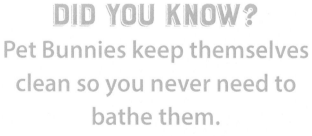

	2 x 2
PINK	x11

DID YOU KNOW?
Pet Bunnies keep themselves clean so you never need to bathe them.

LET'S BUILD BELINDA BUNNY!

1. 1x 2x 1x

2. 1x 1x

3. 1x 2x 2x

4. 1x 1x

5. 4x 8x 8x

6. 4x

HOP-PITI-DOO! ARE YOU READY TO HOP WITH BELINDA BUNNY? LET'S GO!

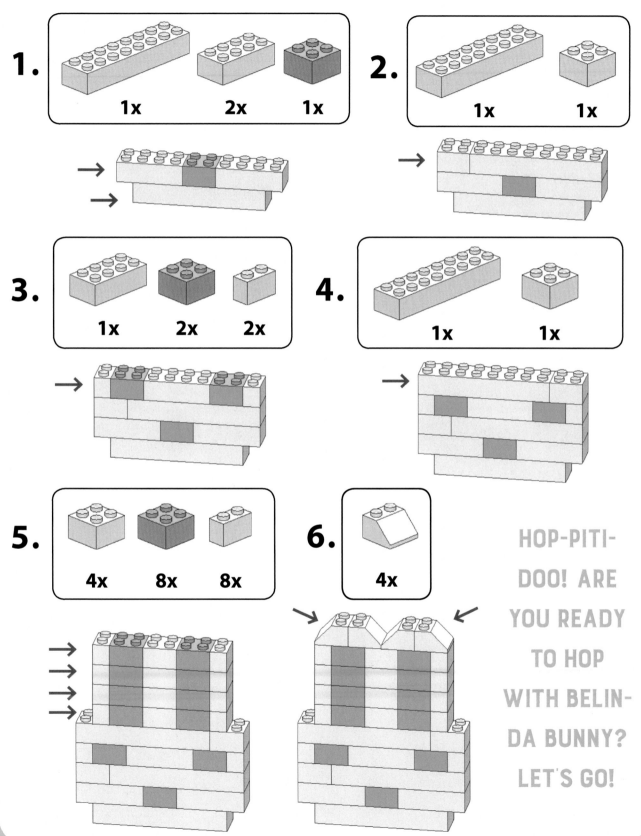

THOMAS TURTLE

Level: EASY

LEARNING CONCEPTS

1. Sort building bricks by color

2. Describe color groups using the words "Dark" and "Light"

3. Follow directions using the words "Top," "Bottom," and "Next to"

READY... GET SET... SORT!

BROWN

2 x 8	2 x 2	1 x 2	2 x 2 SLOPE	2 x 3 SLOPE
x1	x2	x6	x2	x2

GREEN

2 x 2	1 x 2	2 x 2 SLOPE	2 x 3 SLOPE	2 x 2 SLOPE INVERTED
x1	x4	x1	x1	x1

ORANGE

2 x 2	1 x 2
x1	x6

DID YOU KNOW?

Turtles are the only reptiles that have shells.

LET'S BUILD THOMAS TURTLE!

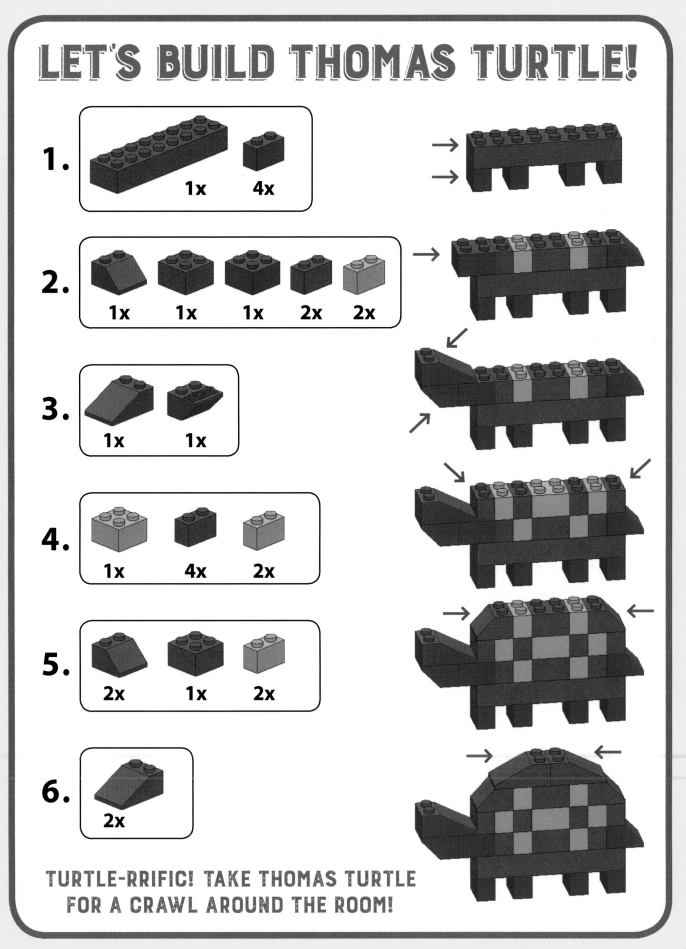

1. 1x 4x

2. 1x 1x 1x 2x 2x

3. 1x 1x

4. 1x 4x 2x

5. 2x 1x 2x

6. 2x

TURTLE-RRIFIC! TAKE THOMAS TURTLE FOR A CRAWL AROUND THE ROOM!

SASHA SNAIL

Level: EASY

LEARNING CONCEPTS

1. Use the words "Same" and "Different" to sort by color

2. Count the number of bricks in each color group

3. Follow directions using the words "First" and "Then"

READY... GET SET... SORT!

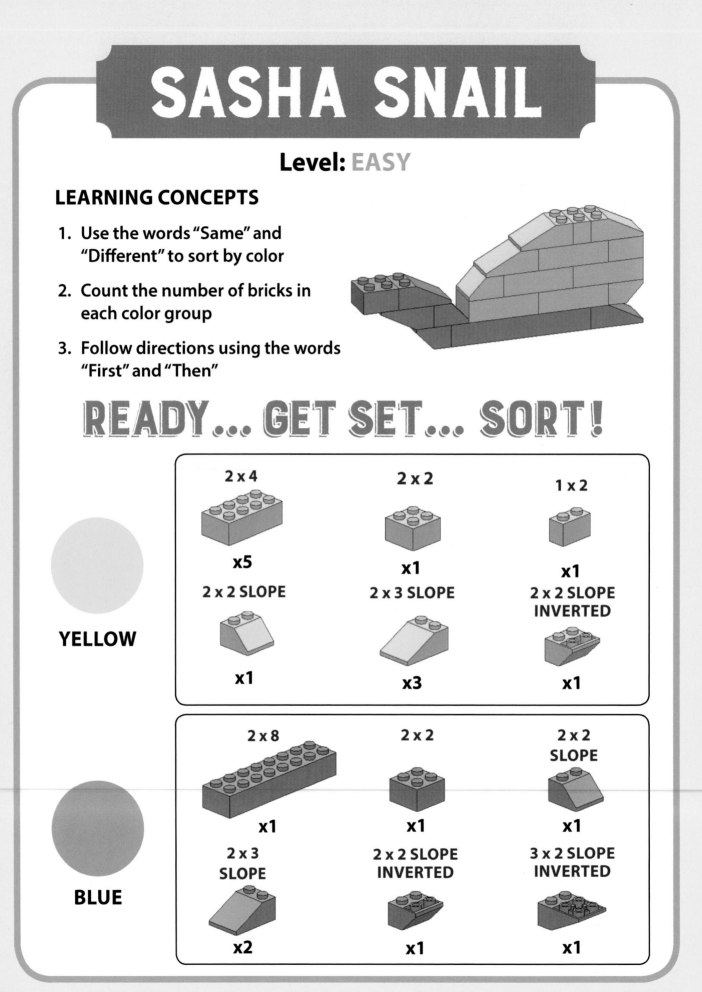

YELLOW

2 x 4
x5

2 x 2
x1

1 x 2
x1

2 x 2 SLOPE
x1

2 x 3 SLOPE
x3

2 x 2 SLOPE INVERTED
x1

BLUE

2 x 8
x1

2 x 2
x1

2 x 2 SLOPE
x1

2 x 3 SLOPE
x2

2 x 2 SLOPE INVERTED
x1

3 x 2 SLOPE INVERTED
x1

LET'S BUILD SASHA SNAIL!

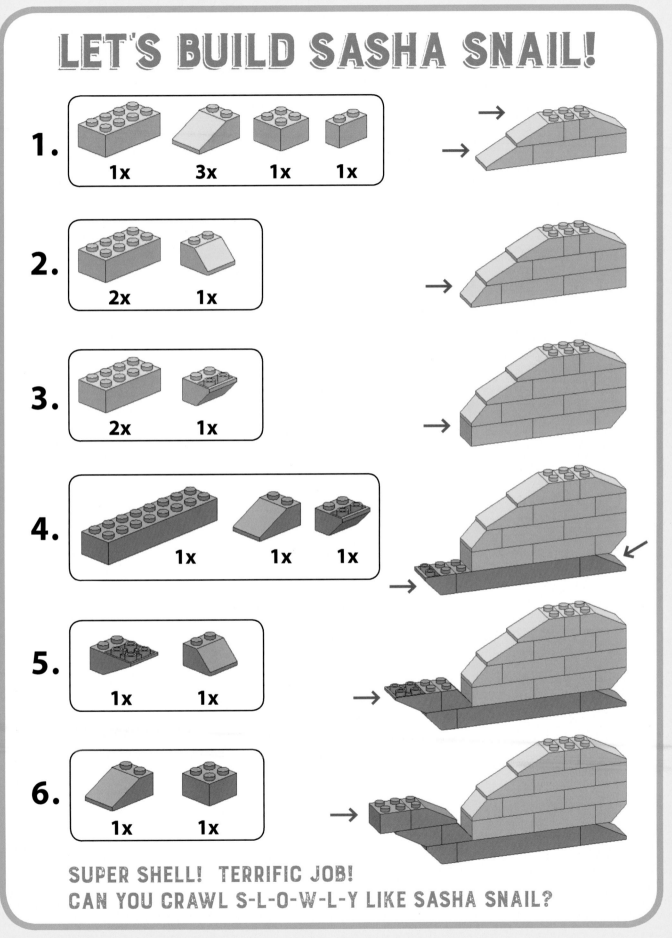

1. 1x 3x 1x 1x

2. 2x 1x

3. 2x 1x

4. 1x 1x 1x

5. 1x 1x

6. 1x 1x

SUPER SHELL! TERRIFIC JOB!
CAN YOU CRAWL S-L-O-W-L-Y LIKE SASHA SNAIL?

MARKY MOUSE

Level: MEDIUM

LEARNING CONCEPTS

1. Sort & group common objects by color, shape, and size

2. Discuss about color gradation concept

3. Find the following shapes: Round, Square, and Rectangle

READY... GET SET... SORT!

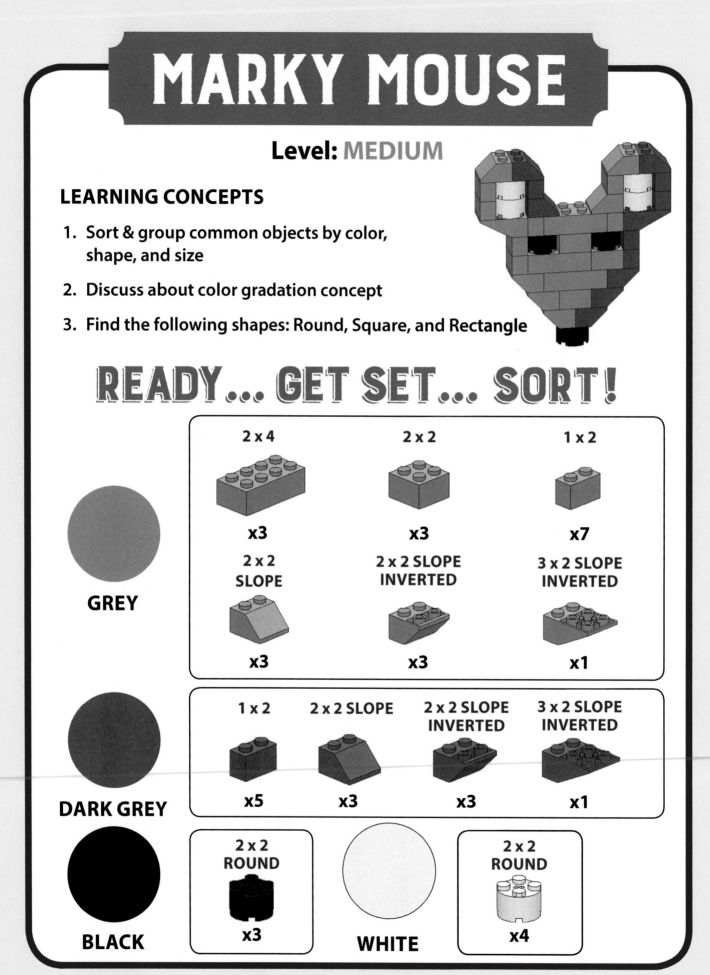

GREY

2 x 4	2 x 2	1 x 2
x3	x3	x7
2 x 2 SLOPE	2 x 2 SLOPE INVERTED	3 x 2 SLOPE INVERTED
x3	x3	x1

DARK GREY

1 x 2	2 x 2 SLOPE	2 x 2 SLOPE INVERTED	3 x 2 SLOPE INVERTED
x5	x3	x3	x1

BLACK

2 x 2 ROUND
x3

WHITE

2 x 2 ROUND
x4

LET'S BUILD MARKY MOUSE!

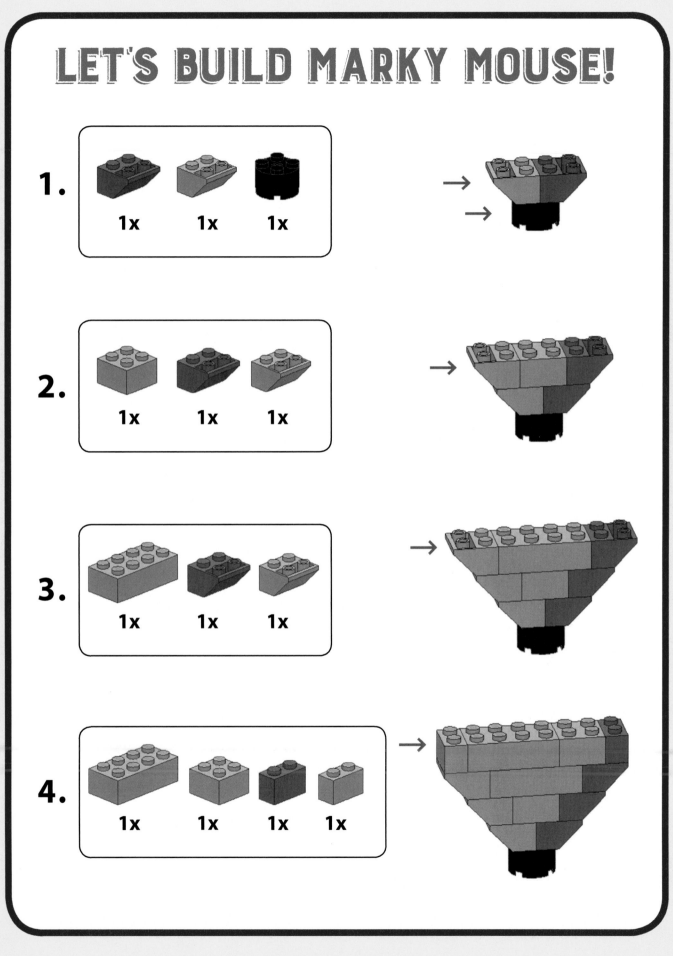

1. 1x 1x 1x

2. 1x 1x 1x

3. 1x 1x 1x

4. 1x 1x 1x 1x

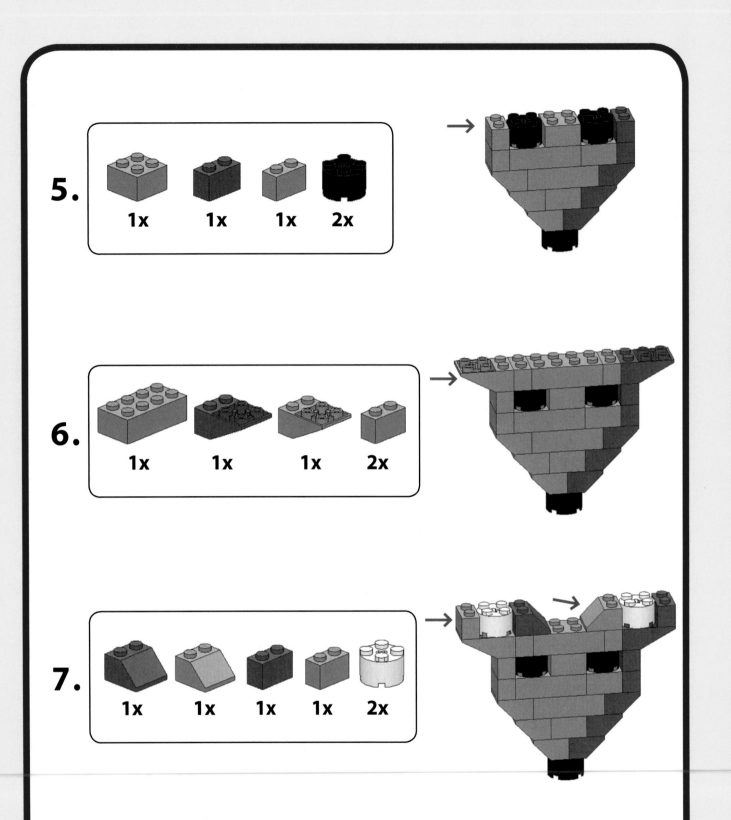

5.

1x 1x 1x 2x

6.

1x 1x 1x 2x

7.

1x 1x 1x 1x 2x

DID YOU KNOW?

The mouse has very bad eyesight! So it uses its
excellent sense of smell to search for its food.

8.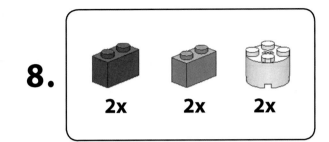

2x   2x   2x

9.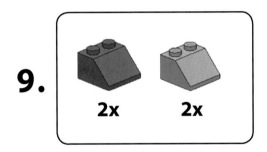

2x   2x

SQUEAK-SQUEAK!
YOU DID GREAT!
MARKY MOUSE LIKES TO
PLAY HIDE AND SEEK.
WHERE SHOULD HE HIDE?

CATRINA CAT

Level: MEDIUM

LEARNING CONCEPTS

1. Sort & group common objects by color, shape, and size

2. Describe each color group using comparison words such as "More" and "Most"

3. Compare bricks that are "Long" and "Short"

READY... GET SET... SORT!

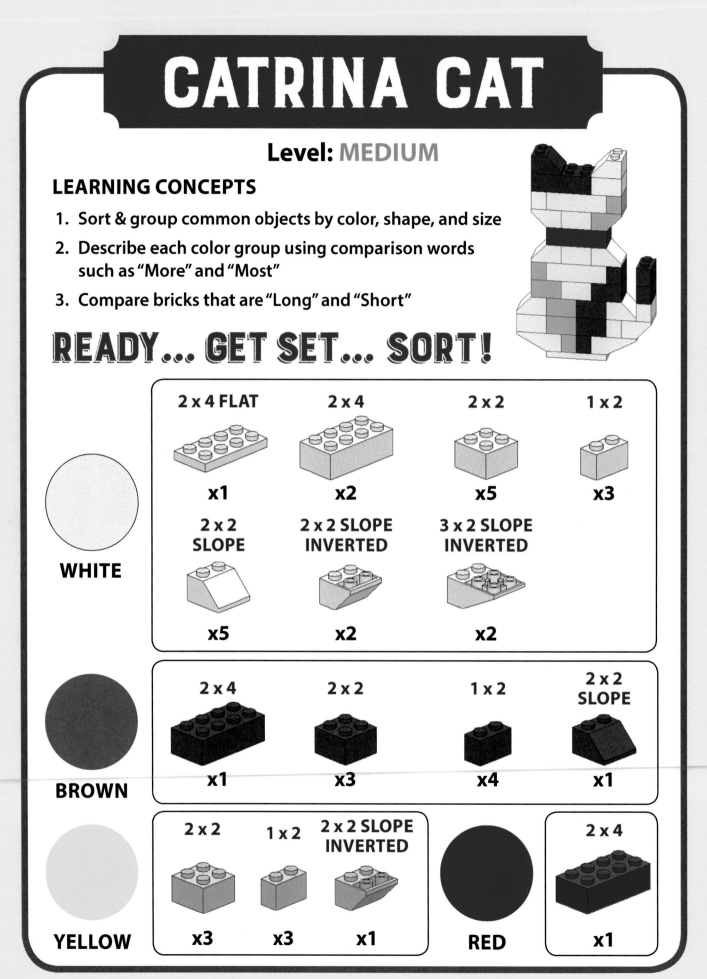

WHITE

2 x 4 FLAT	2 x 4	2 x 2	1 x 2
x1	x2	x5	x3

2 x 2 SLOPE	2 x 2 SLOPE INVERTED	3 x 2 SLOPE INVERTED
x5	x2	x2

BROWN

2 x 4	2 x 2	1 x 2	2 x 2 SLOPE
x1	x3	x4	x1

YELLOW

2 x 2	1 x 2	2 x 2 SLOPE INVERTED
x3	x3	x1

RED

2 x 4
x1

LET'S BUILD CATRINA CAT!

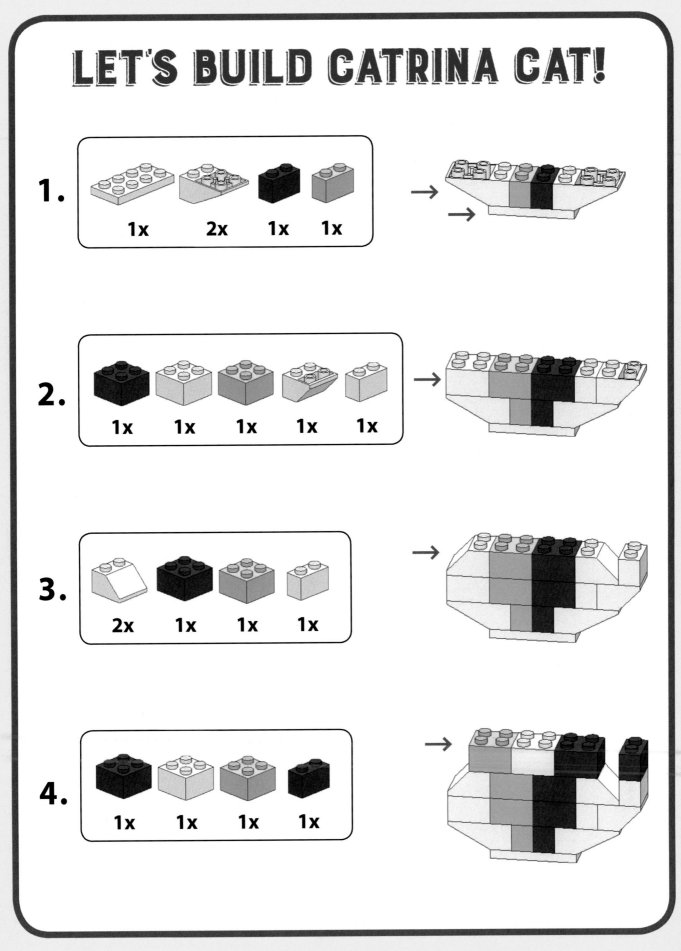

1. 1x 2x 1x 1x

2. 1x 1x 1x 1x 1x

3. 2x 1x 1x 1x

4. 1x 1x 1x 1x

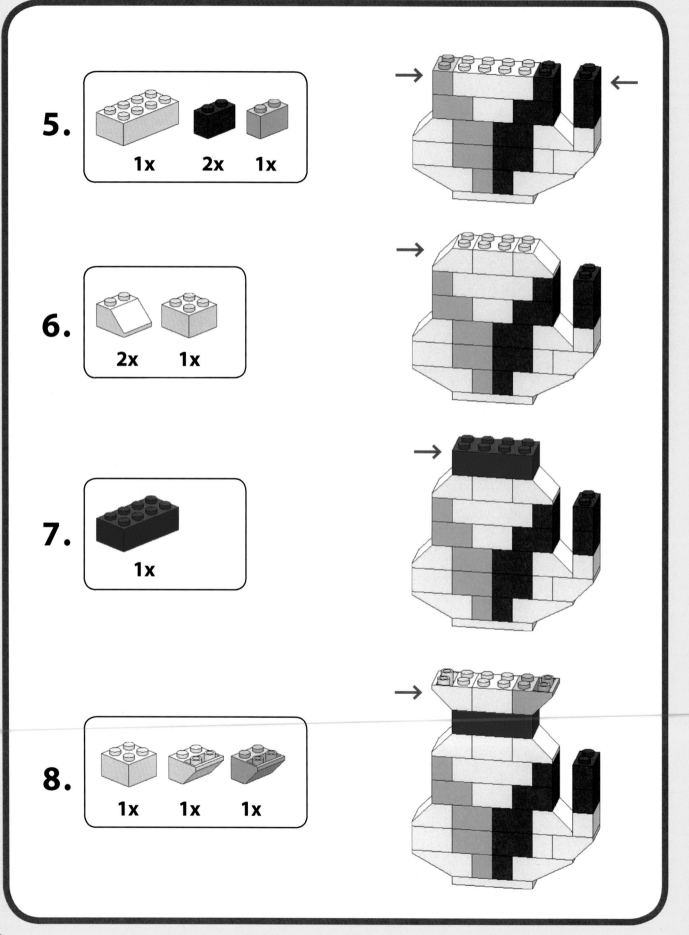

5. 1x 2x 1x

6. 2x 1x

7. 1x

8. 1x 1x 1x

9.

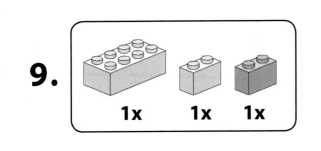

1x   1x   1x

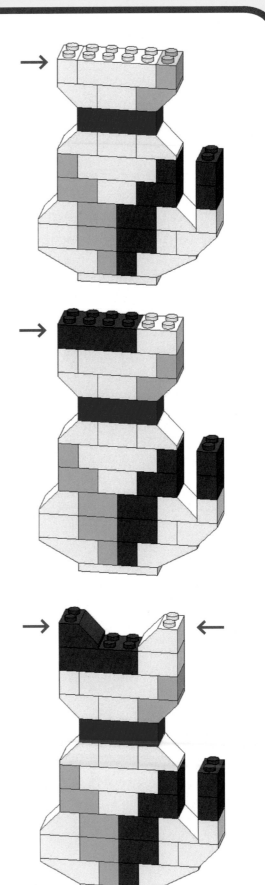

10.

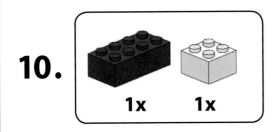

1x   1x

11.

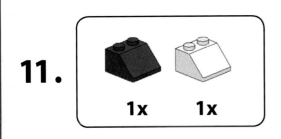

1x   1x

MEOW-MEOW MAGNIFICENT! WHAT DOES CATRINA CAT LIKE TO PLAY WITH?

DONNY DOG

Level: MEDIUM

LEARNING CONCEPTS

1. Sort & group common objects by color, shape, and size

2. Compare bricks using the words "Longer" and "Shorter"

3. Follow directions using the words "First," "Second," and "Third"

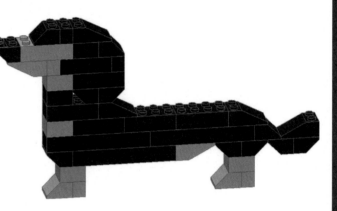

READY... GET SET... SORT!

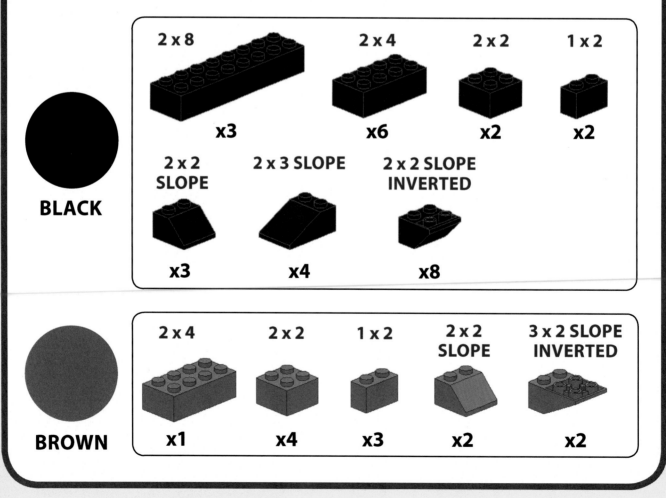

BLACK

2 x 8	2 x 4	2 x 2	1 x 2
x3	x6	x2	x2

2 x 2 SLOPE	2 x 3 SLOPE	2 x 2 SLOPE INVERTED
x3	x4	x8

BROWN

2 x 4	2 x 2	1 x 2	2 x 2 SLOPE	3 x 2 SLOPE INVERTED
x1	x4	x3	x2	x2

LET'S BUILD DONNY DOG!

1. 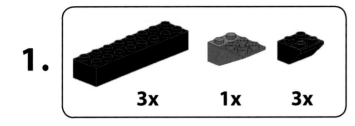 3x 1x 3x

2.  2x

3. 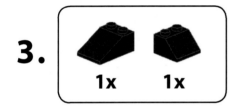 1x 1x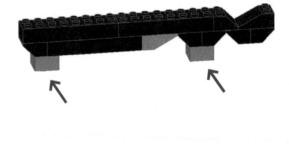

4. 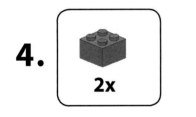 2x

5. 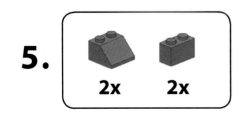 2x 2x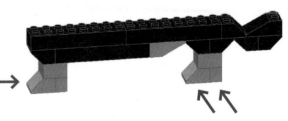

6. 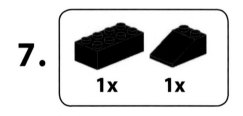 3x 1x 1x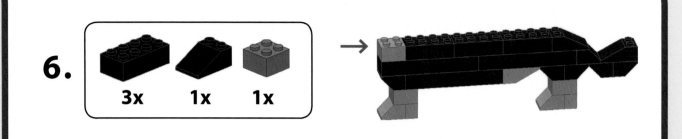

7. 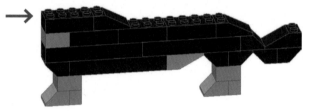 1x 1x

8. 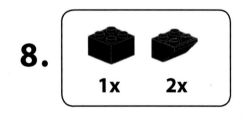 1x 2x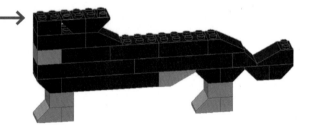

9. 1x 1x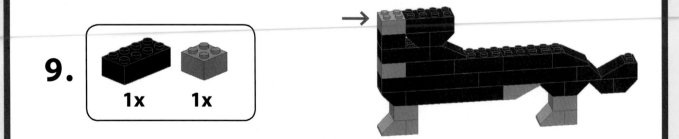

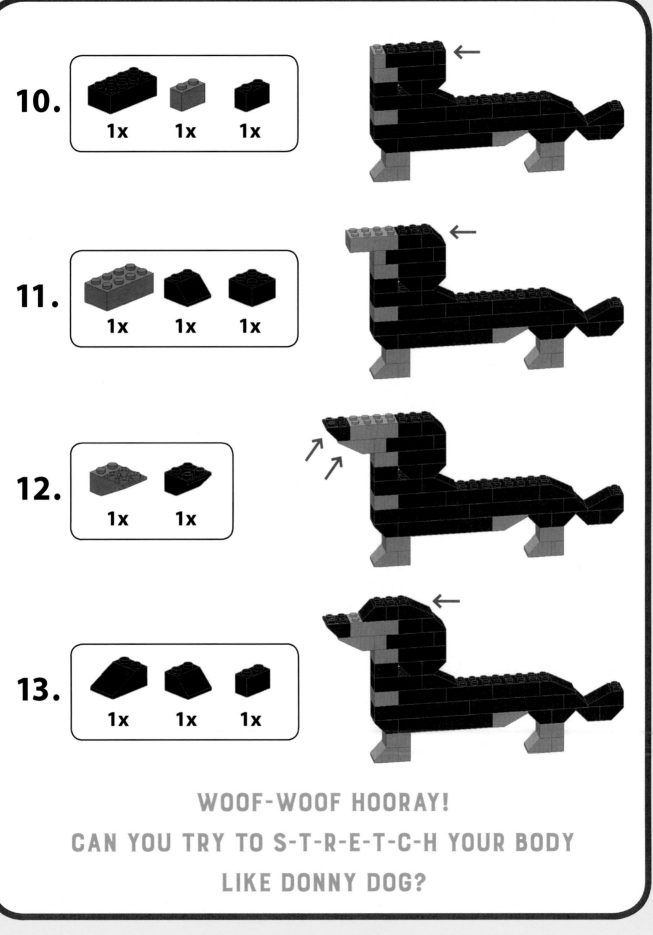

10. 1x 1x 1x

11. 1x 1x 1x

12. 1x 1x

13. 1x 1x 1x

WOOF-WOOF HOORAY!
CAN YOU TRY TO S-T-R-E-T-C-H YOUR BODY
LIKE DONNY DOG?

GORDON GOLDFISH

Level: MEDIUM

LEARNING CONCEPTS

1. Sort & group common objects by color, shape, and size

2. Compare bricks using the words "Bigger" and "Smaller"

3. Stack 3 different colored bricks and identify "Top," "Middle," and "Bottom"

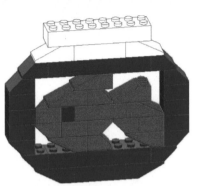

READY... GET SET... SORT!

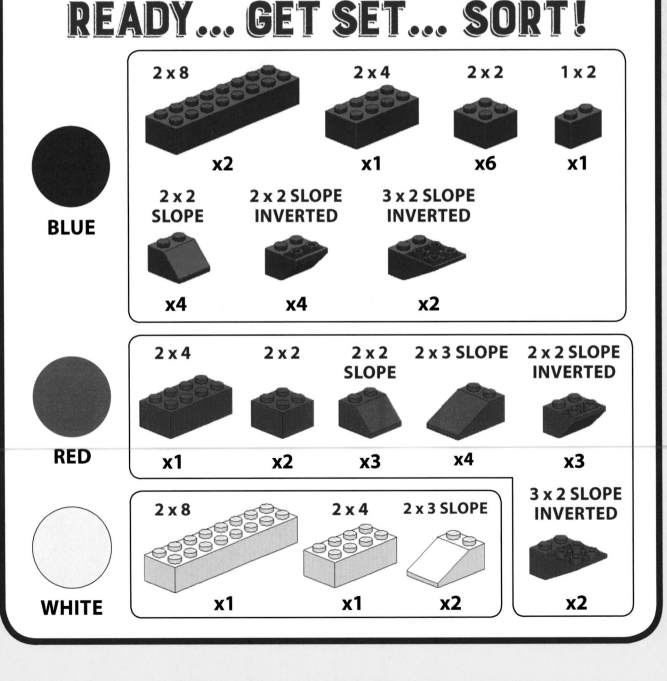

BLUE

2 x 8	2 x 4	2 x 2	1 x 2
x2	x1	x6	x1

2 x 2 SLOPE	2 x 2 SLOPE INVERTED	3 x 2 SLOPE INVERTED
x4	x4	x2

RED

2 x 4	2 x 2	2 x 2 SLOPE	2 x 3 SLOPE	2 x 2 SLOPE INVERTED
x1	x2	x3	x4	x3

WHITE

2 x 8	2 x 4	2 x 3 SLOPE	3 x 2 SLOPE INVERTED
x1	x1	x2	x2

LET'S BUILD GORDON GOLDFISH!

1.
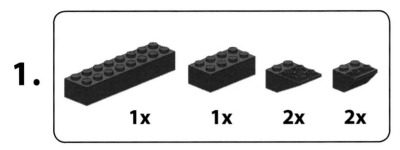
1x   1x   2x   2x

2.
2x   1x   2x
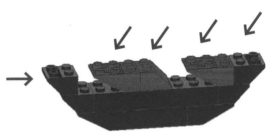

3.
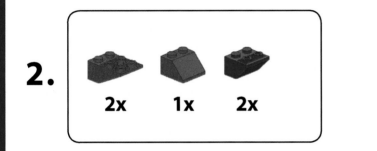
2x   2x   3x

4.
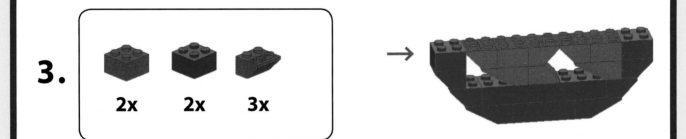
1x   1x   1x   2x   1x

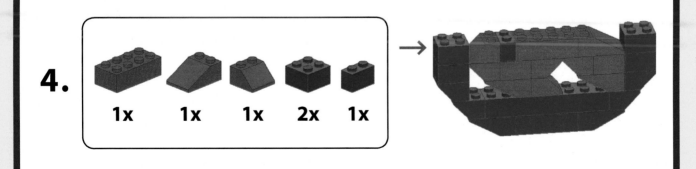

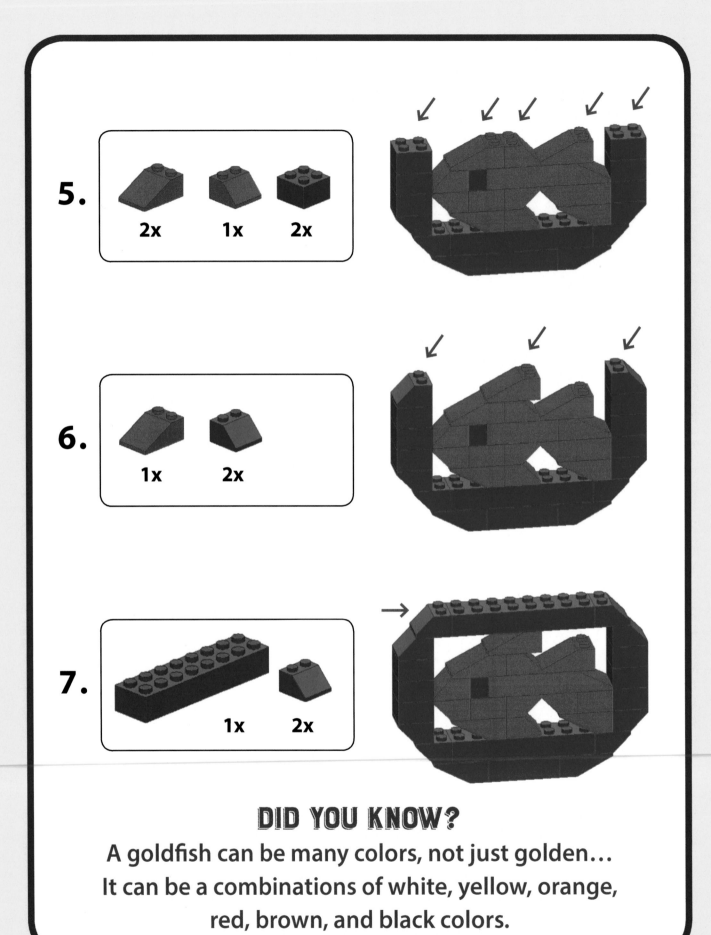

5. 2x 1x 2x

6. 1x 2x

7. 1x 2x

DID YOU KNOW?
A goldfish can be many colors, not just golden…
It can be a combinations of white, yellow, orange,
red, brown, and black colors.

8. 1x 2x

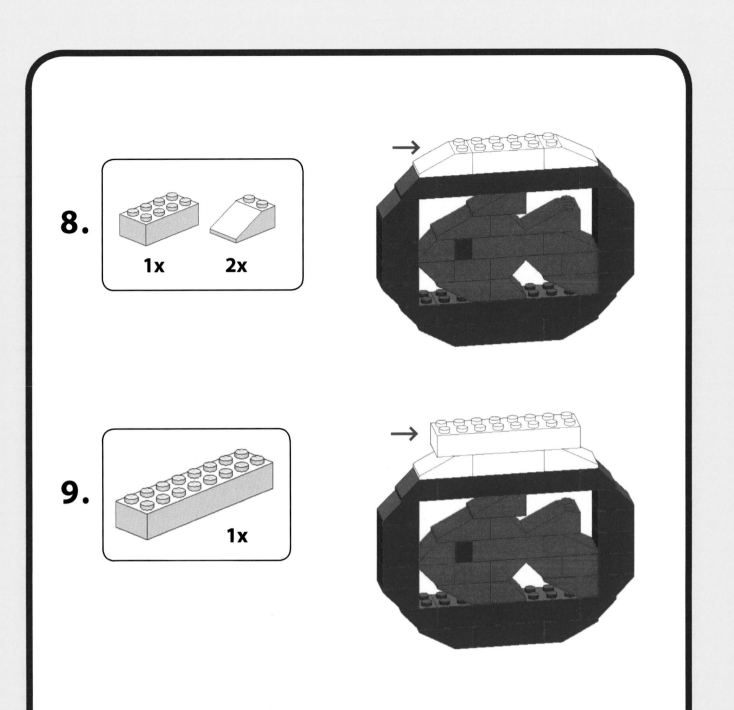

9. 1x

SWISHY JOB!
GORDON GOLDFISH IS FEELING HUNGRY.
WHAT SHOULD HE EAT?

SEYMOUR SNAKE

Level: ADVANCED

LEARNING CONCEPTS

1. Sort & group common objects by color, shape, and size

2. Understand the concepts of "More" and "Most"

3. Follow directions using the words "On Top" and "Under"

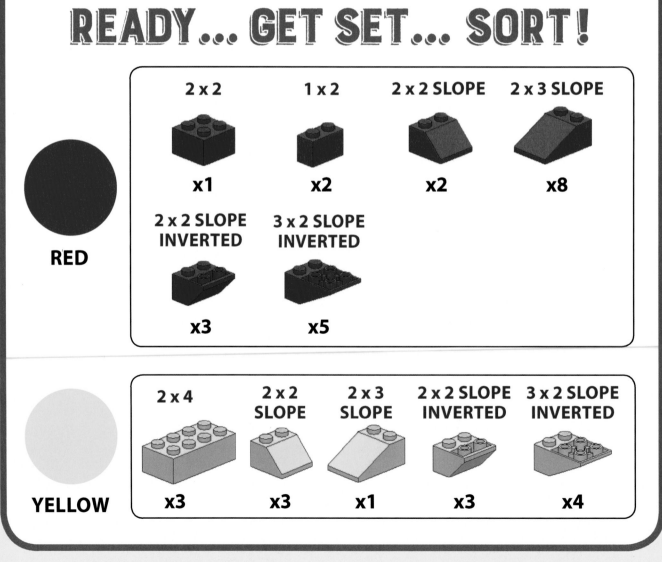

READY... GET SET... SORT!

RED

2 x 2	1 x 2	2 x 2 SLOPE	2 x 3 SLOPE
x1	x2	x2	x8

2 x 2 SLOPE INVERTED	3 x 2 SLOPE INVERTED
x3	x5

YELLOW

2 x 4	2 x 2 SLOPE	2 x 3 SLOPE	2 x 2 SLOPE INVERTED	3 x 2 SLOPE INVERTED
x3	x3	x1	x3	x4

LET'S BUILD SEYMOUR SNAKE!

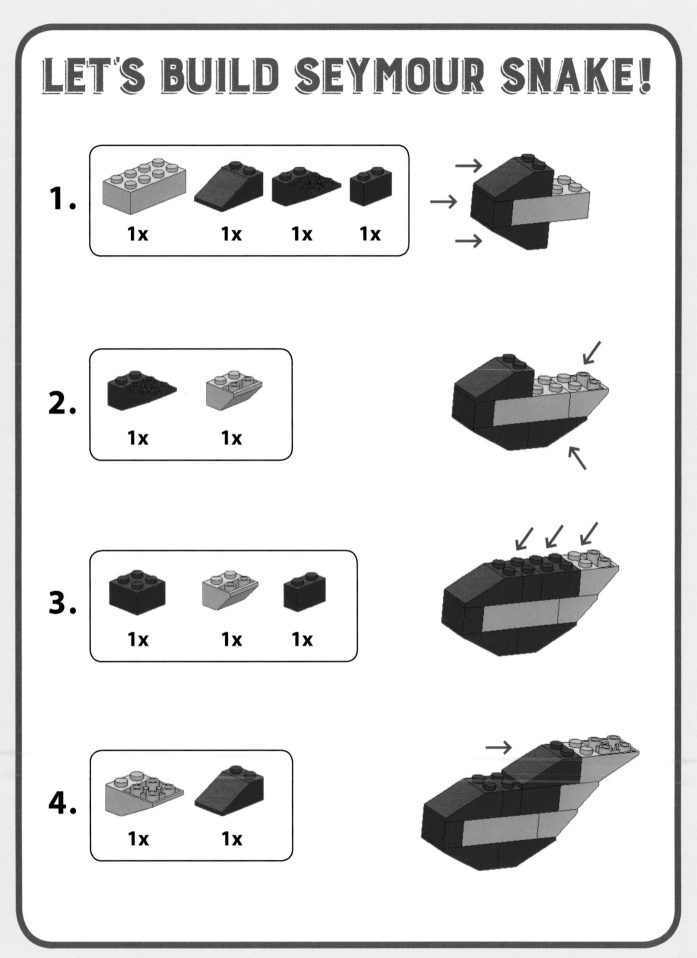

1. 1x 1x 1x 1x

2. 1x 1x

3. 1x 1x 1x

4. 1x 1x

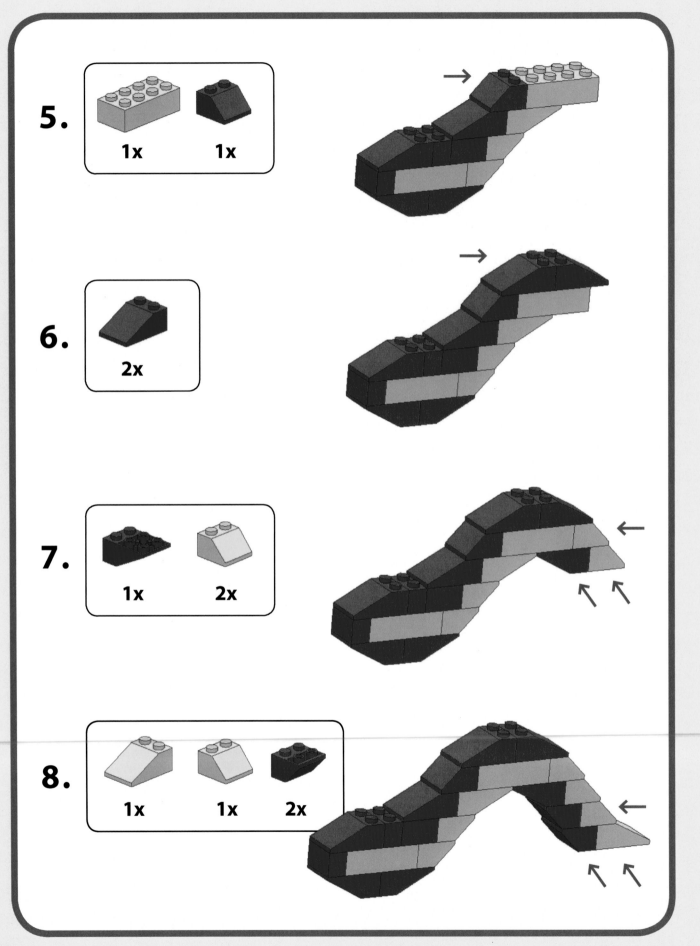

5. 1x 1x

6. 2x

7. 1x 2x

8. 1x 1x 2x

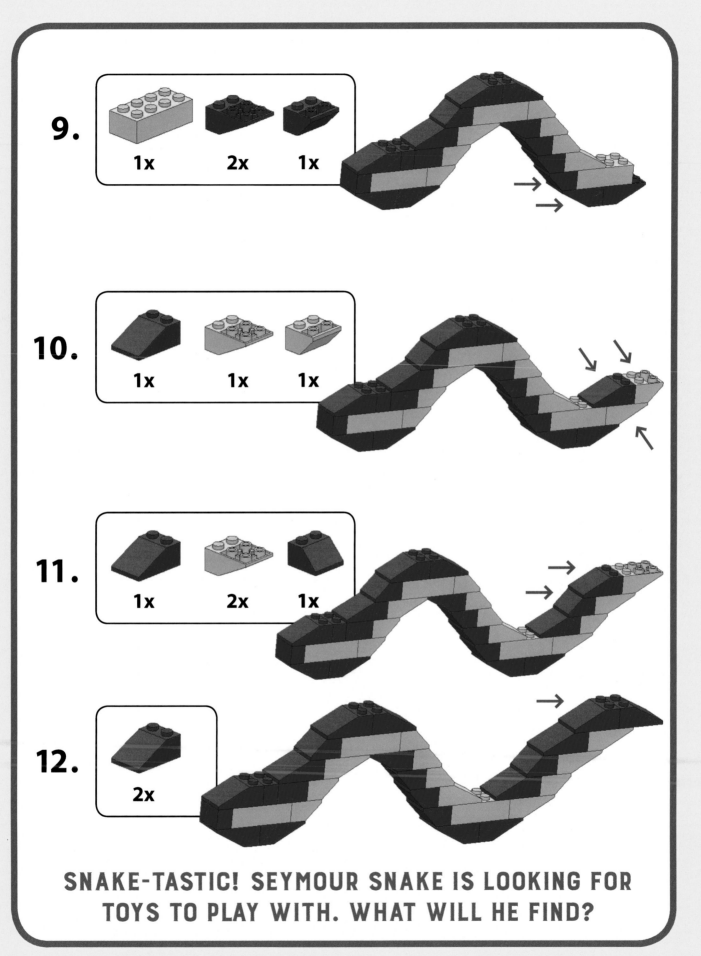

SNAKE-TASTIC! SEYMOUR SNAKE IS LOOKING FOR TOYS TO PLAY WITH. WHAT WILL HE FIND?

PATTY PARROT

Level: ADVANCED

LEARNING CONCEPTS

1. Sort & group common objects by color, shape, and size

2. Recognize sloping shapes

3. Follow directions using the words "Top," "Bottom," and "Next to"

READY... GET SET... SORT!

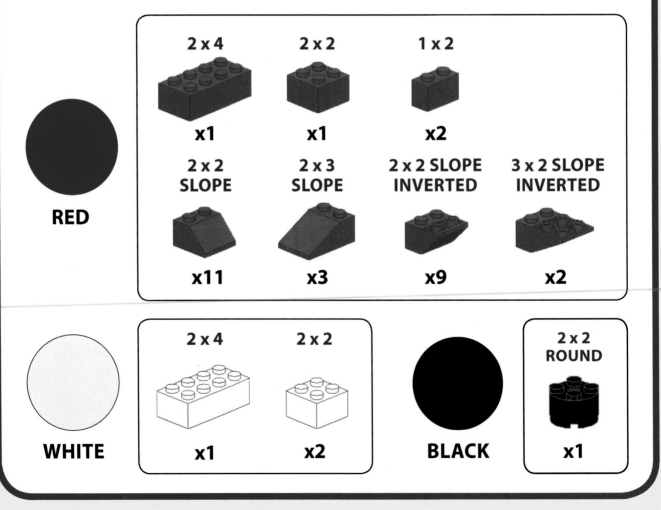

RED

2 x 4	2 x 2	1 x 2
x1	x1	x2

2 x 2 SLOPE	2 x 3 SLOPE	2 x 2 SLOPE INVERTED	3 x 2 SLOPE INVERTED
x11	x3	x9	x2

WHITE

2 x 4	2 x 2
x1	x2

BLACK

2 x 2 ROUND

x1

LIGHT BLUE

2 x 4	2 x 2	1 x 2
x4	x1	x1

2 x 2 SLOPE	2 x 3 SLOPE	2 x 2 SLOPE INVERTED	3 x 2 SLOPE INVERTED
x1	x2	x2	x2

YELLOW

2 x 4	2 x 2	1 x 2	2 x 2 SLOPE	2 x 2 SLOPE INVERTED
x1	x4	x4	x5	x3

LET'S BUILD PATTY PARROT!

1.
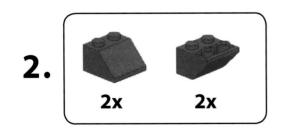
1x 1x 1x
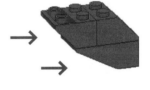

2.
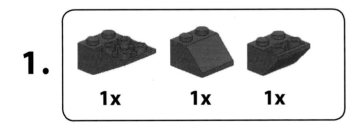
2x 2x
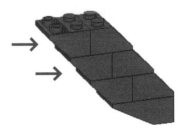

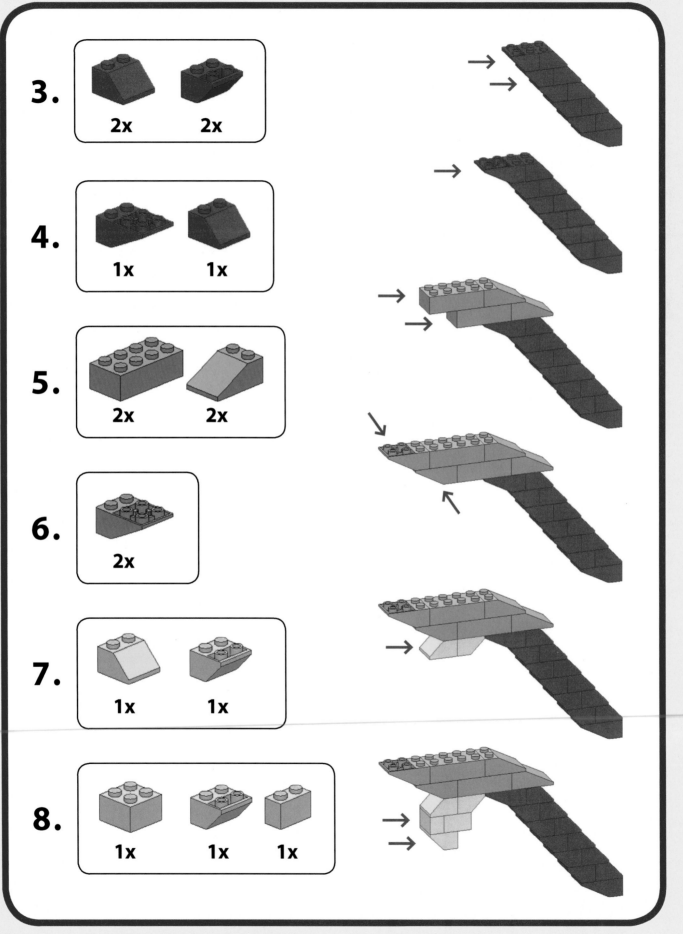

3. 2x 2x

4. 1x 1x

5. 2x 2x

6. 2x

7. 1x 1x

8. 1x 1x 1x

9.

1x 1x 1x 1x

10.

1x 1x 1x 1x

11.

1x 1x 1x 1x 1x

12.

1x 1x 1x 1x

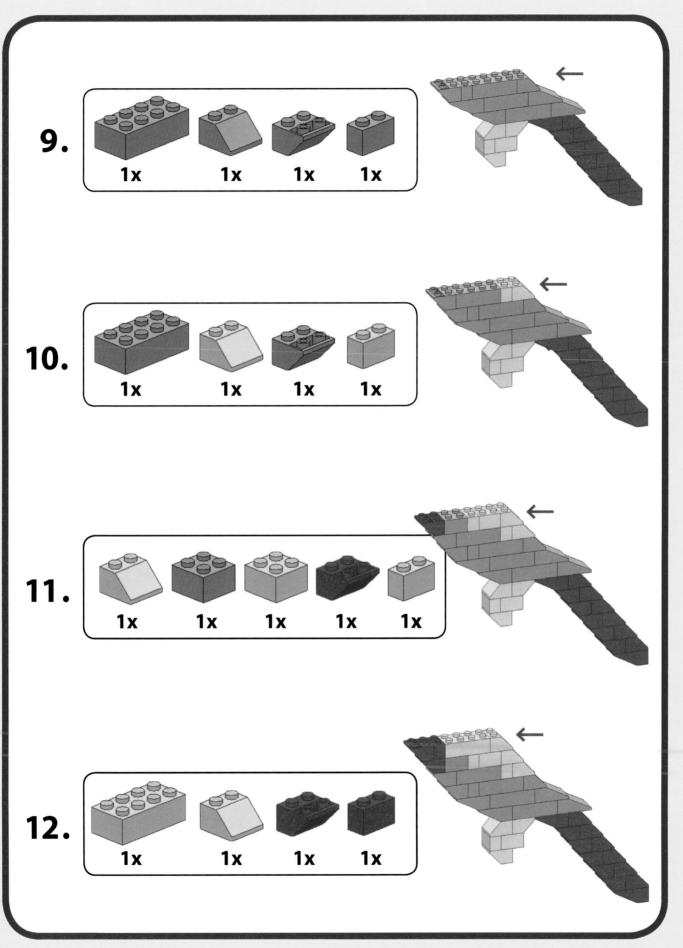

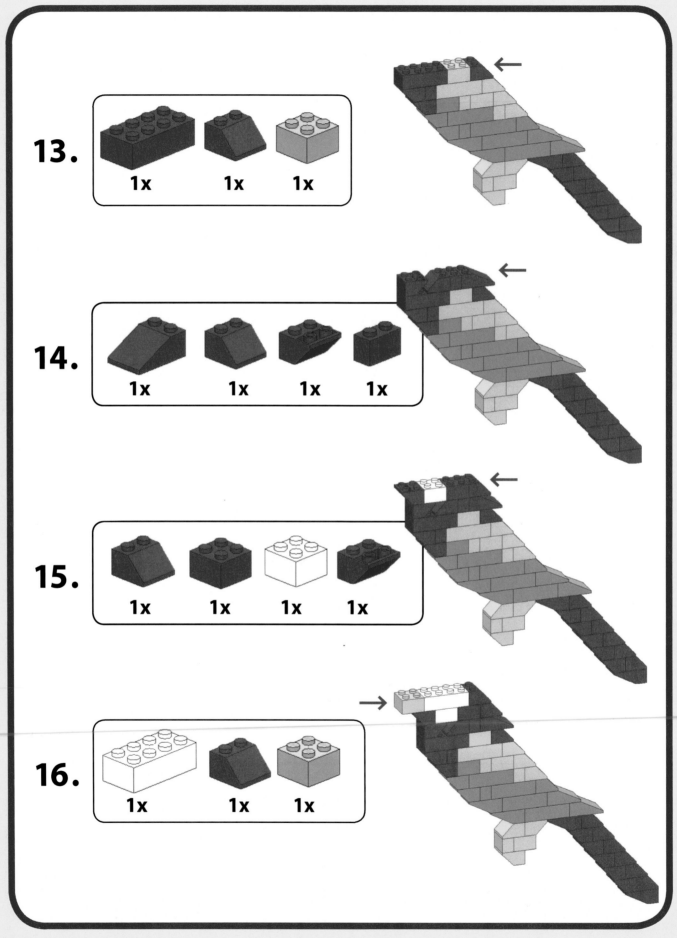

13. 1x 1x 1x

14. 1x 1x 1x 1x

15. 1x 1x 1x 1x

16. 1x 1x 1x

17.

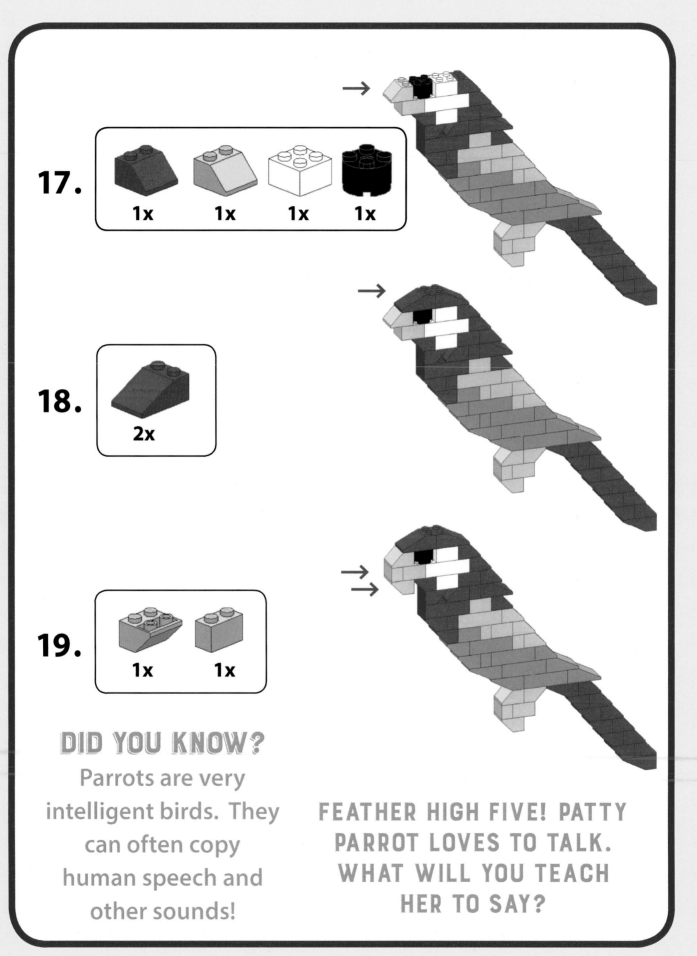

1x   1x   1x   1x

18.

2x

19.

1x   1x

DID YOU KNOW?

Parrots are very intelligent birds. They can often copy human speech and other sounds!

FEATHER HIGH FIVE! PATTY PARROT LOVES TO TALK. WHAT WILL YOU TEACH HER TO SAY?

ABOUT THE AUTHORS

DESIGNER PAUL BACIO and editorial reviewer Elaine Bacio have three kids—Caleb, Joy, and Abby—who absolutely *love* brick-building. Paul, a former youth pastor and brick-building summer camp curriculum developer, is always inspiring his children and students to branch out into building imaginative new sets and ideas. Elaine is a certified health coach and a homeschooling mom. The couple live with their children in San Mateo, California.

CO-DESIGNER SOFIA CHEN is a fourth grader at Hugo Reid Elementary School. Sofia loves playing brick-building with Natalie, her little sister, after school—every day. Besides playing with bricks, Sofia also enjoys drawing, playing the piano and the viola, gardening, and helping her mom fundraise money for special-needs children. She lives with her parents, project editor Ann Kositchotitana and her husband, Ronald Chen, and her little sister, Natalie, in Arcadia, California.